Garfield makes it big

BY: JIM DAVIS

BALLANTINE BOOKS · NEW YORK

Published in the United States by Ballantine Books, a division of Random House, Inc., New York, and simultaneously in Canada by Random House of Canada Limited, Toronto.

Library of Congress Catalog Card Number: 84-91658
ISBN 0-345-31982-1

Manufactured in the United States of America

First Edition: March 1985

10 9 8 7 6 5 4 3 2 1

The Big Cheese, The Head
Honcho, The Chief Muckamuck...

NEWS FLASH!
Jim Davis a Fraud!

Teddy bear Pooky recently revealed that Jim Davis did not create the Garfield comic strip. Garfield himself writes and draws the world-famous cartoon. Garfield has been sitting at a drawing board for the last six years as Davis has gained notoriety through national television and print. Davis was not available for comment, but Garfield was. "The way I figured it, who would ever believe a cat could do a comic strip. So, I hired this down-and-out, hack cartoonist to take the credit for it. Sure ... he looked good and said all the right things, but it's time the truth was known."

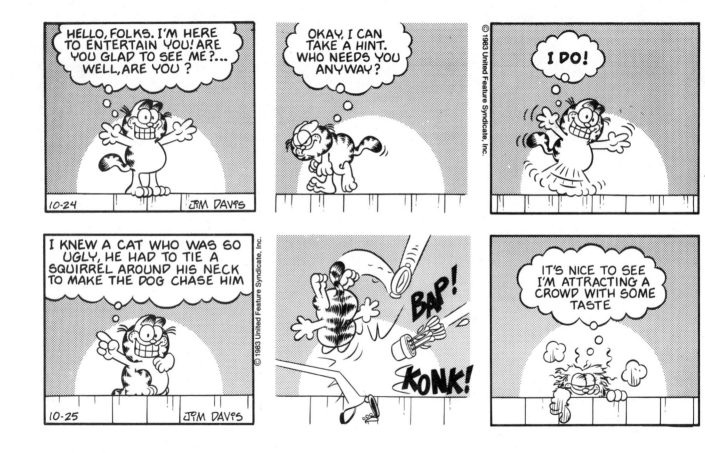

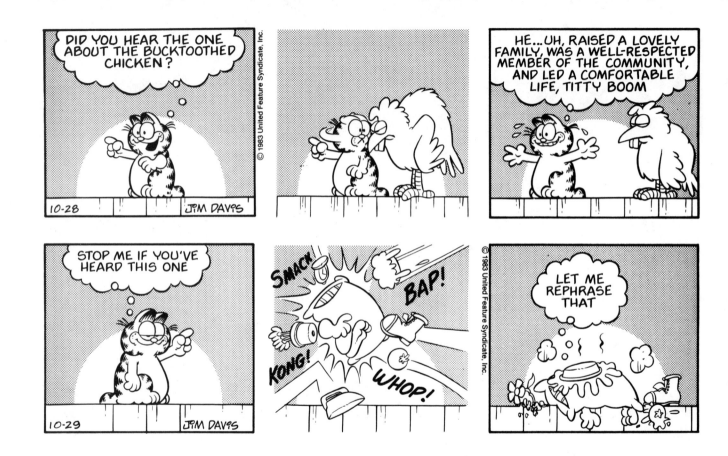

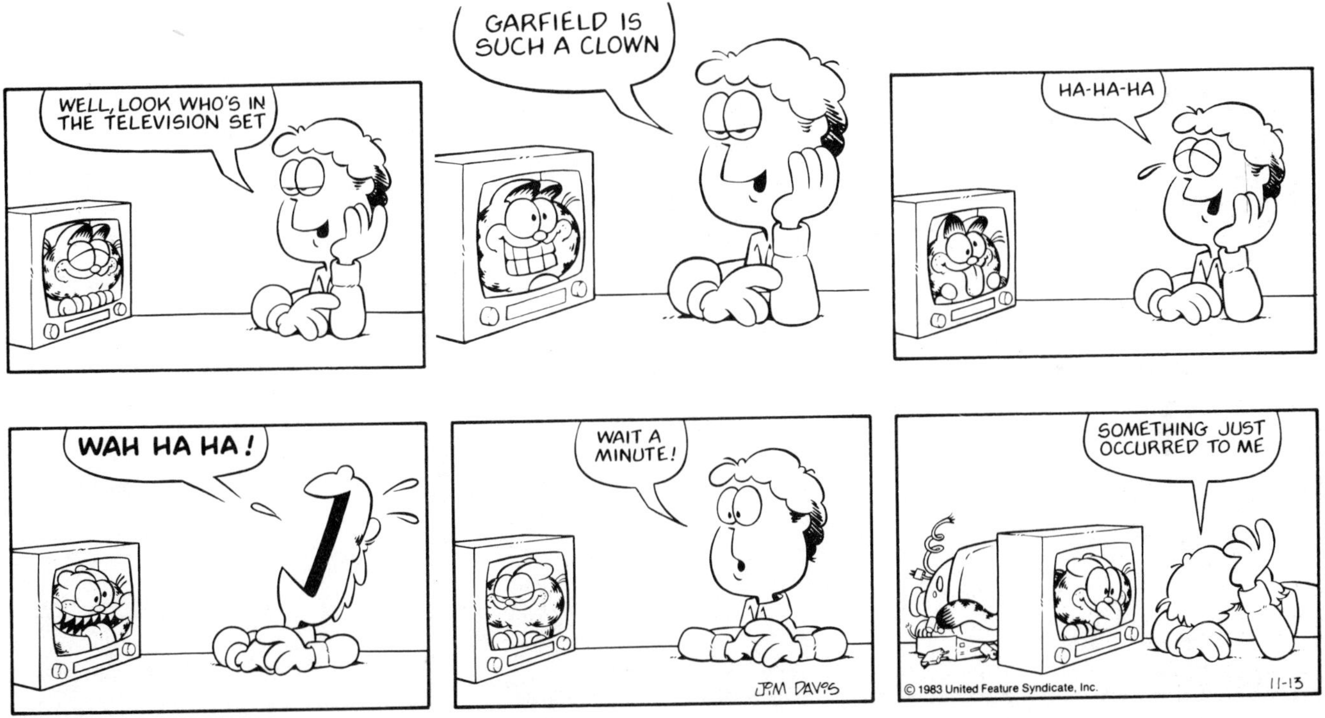
WELL, LOOK WHO'S IN THE TELEVISION SET
GARFIELD IS SUCH A CLOWN
HA-HA-HA
WAH HA HA!
WAIT A MINUTE!
JIM DAVIS
SOMETHING JUST OCCURRED TO ME
© 1983 United Feature Syndicate, Inc.
11-13

© 1983 United Feature Syndicate, Inc.

CLICK *WHIRRR*

GASP!

SPLAT!

HELLO, MOM? THE WASHING MACHINE JUST SPIT OUT MY JOCKEY SHORTS

THAT'S ONE THING I'D NEVER ADMIT TO MY MOTHER

JIM DAVIS 11-20

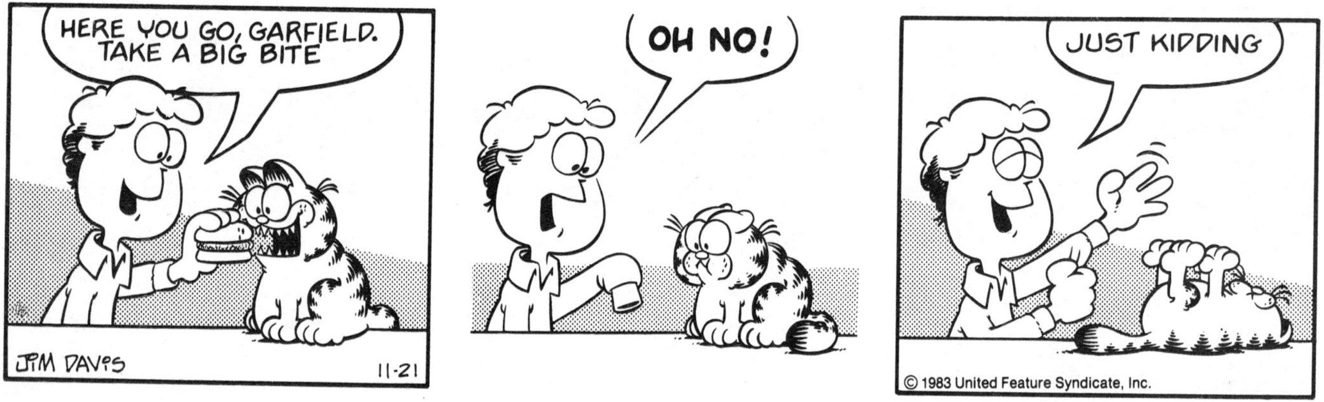
HERE YOU GO, GARFIELD. TAKE A BIG BITE
JIM DAVIS
11-21
OH NO!
JUST KIDDING

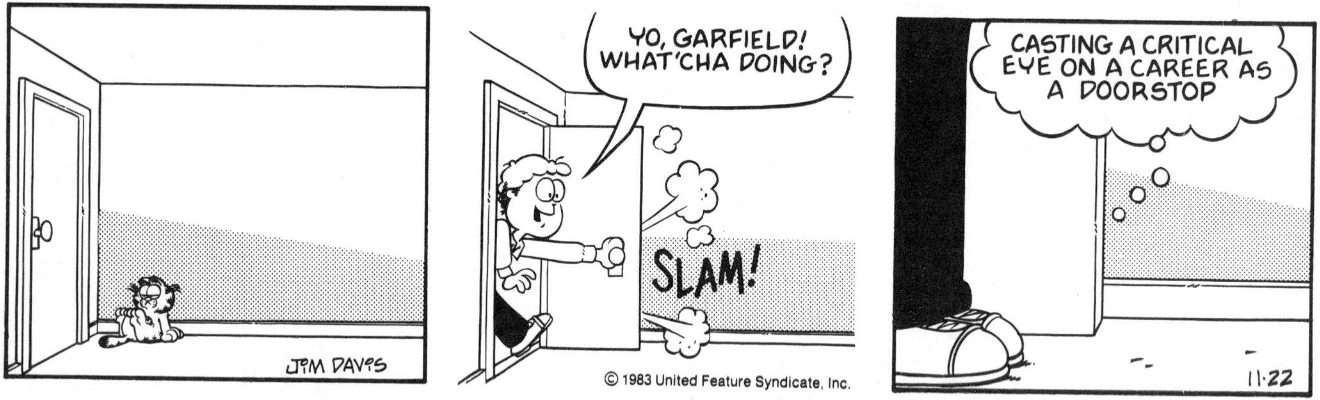
JIM DAVIS
YO, GARFIELD! WHAT'CHA DOING?
SLAM!
CASTING A CRITICAL EYE ON A CAREER AS A DOORSTOP
11·22

THEY DIDN'T CALL ME THE SHIMMY KING FOR NOTHING

JIM DAVIS

11-27

© 1983 United Feature Syndicate, Inc.

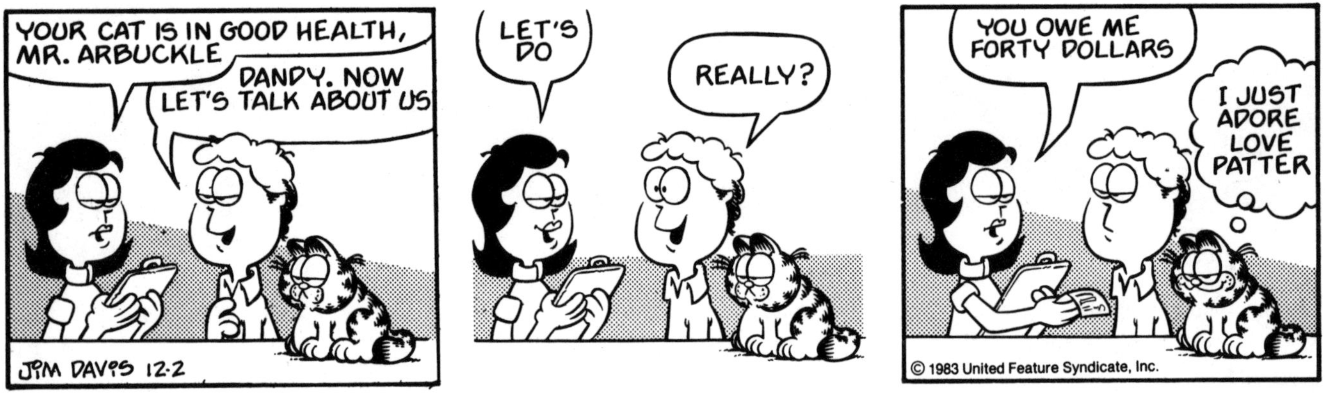
YOUR CAT IS IN GOOD HEALTH, MR. ARBUCKLE
DANDY. NOW LET'S TALK ABOUT US
LET'S DO
REALLY?
YOU OWE ME FORTY DOLLARS
I JUST ADORE LOVE PATTER
JIM DAVIS 12-2
© 1983 United Feature Syndicate, Inc.

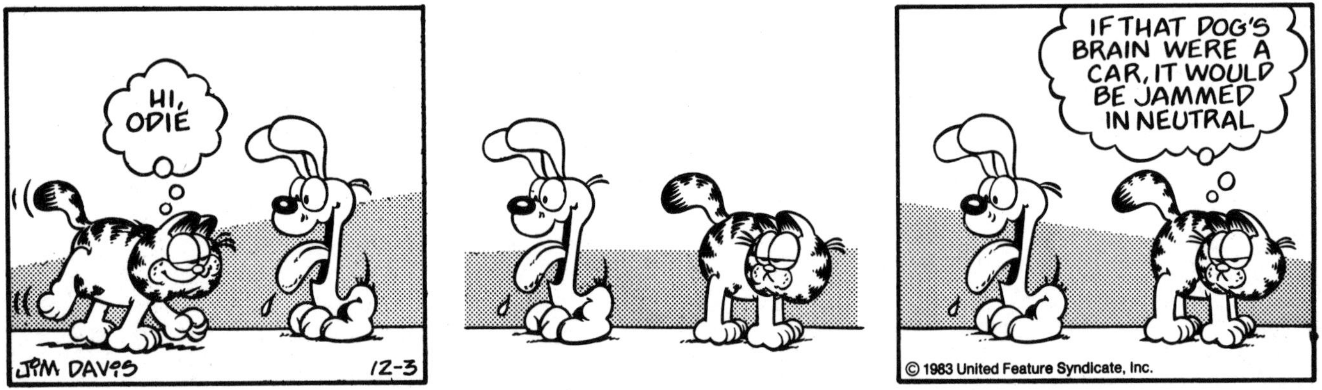
HI, ODIE
IF THAT DOG'S BRAIN WERE A CAR, IT WOULD BE JAMMED IN NEUTRAL
JIM DAVIS 12-3
© 1983 United Feature Syndicate, Inc.

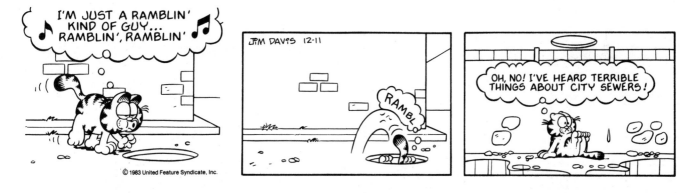

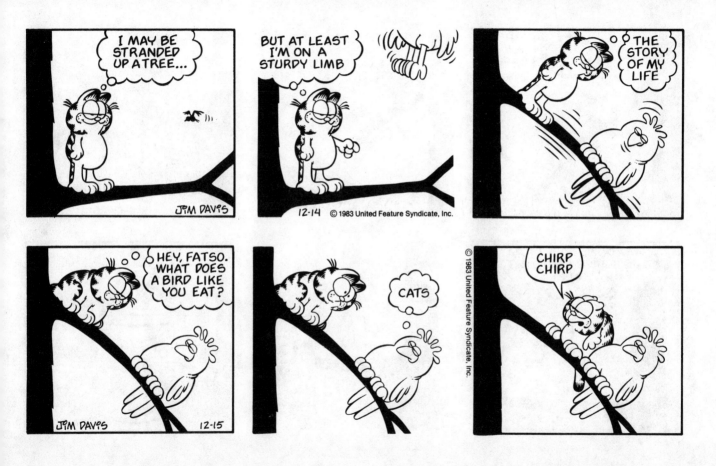

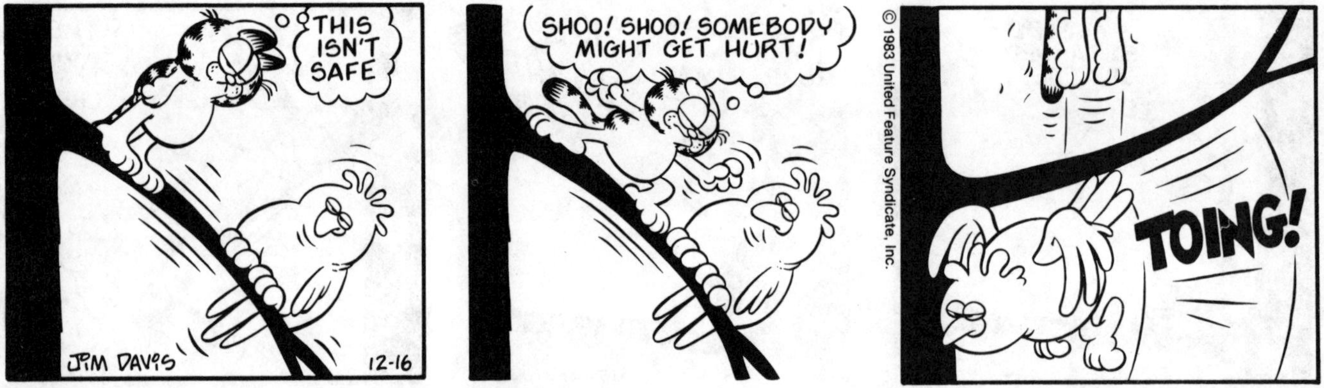
THIS ISN'T SAFE
SHOO! SHOO! SOMEBODY MIGHT GET HURT!
TOING!
JIM DAVIS
12-16
© 1983 United Feature Syndicate, Inc.

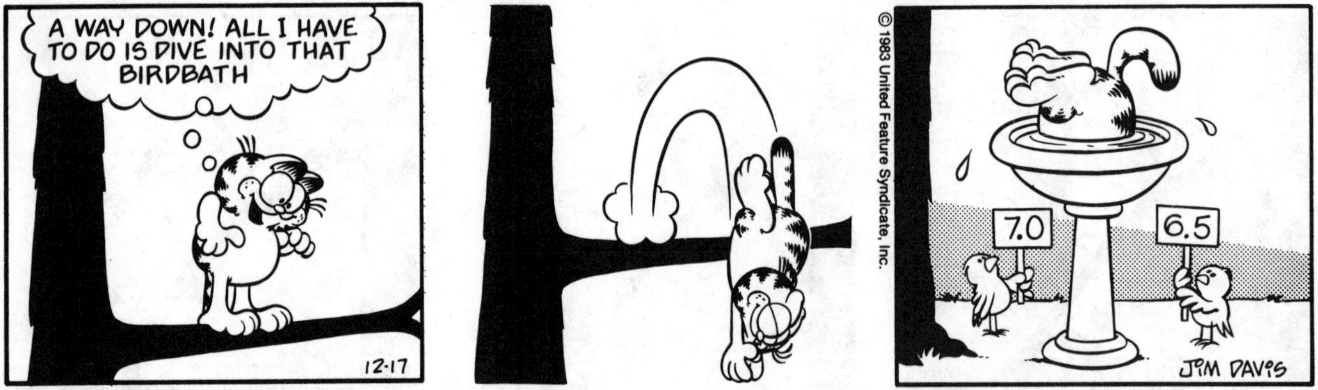
A WAY DOWN! ALL I HAVE TO DO IS DIVE INTO THAT BIRDBATH
7.0
6.5
JIM DAVIS
12-17
© 1983 United Feature Syndicate, Inc.

The stump of a pipe he held tight in his teeth,
And the smoke it encircled his head like a wreath;
He had a broad face and a little round belly
That shook when he laughed, like a bowlful of jelly.

He was chubby and plump, a right jolly old elf,
And I laughed when I saw him, in spite of myself;
A wink of his eye and a twist of his head
Soon gave me to know I had nothing to dread.

He spoke not a word, but went straight to his work,
And filled all the stockings; then turned with a jerk,
And laying his finger aside of his nose,
And giving a nod, up the chimney he rose;

He sprang to his sleigh, to his team gave a whistle,
And away they all flew like the down of a thistle.
But I heard him exclaim, ere he drove out of sight,

HAPPY CHRISTMAS TO ALL AND TO ALL A GOOD NIGHT!

JIM DAVIS

1-8-84

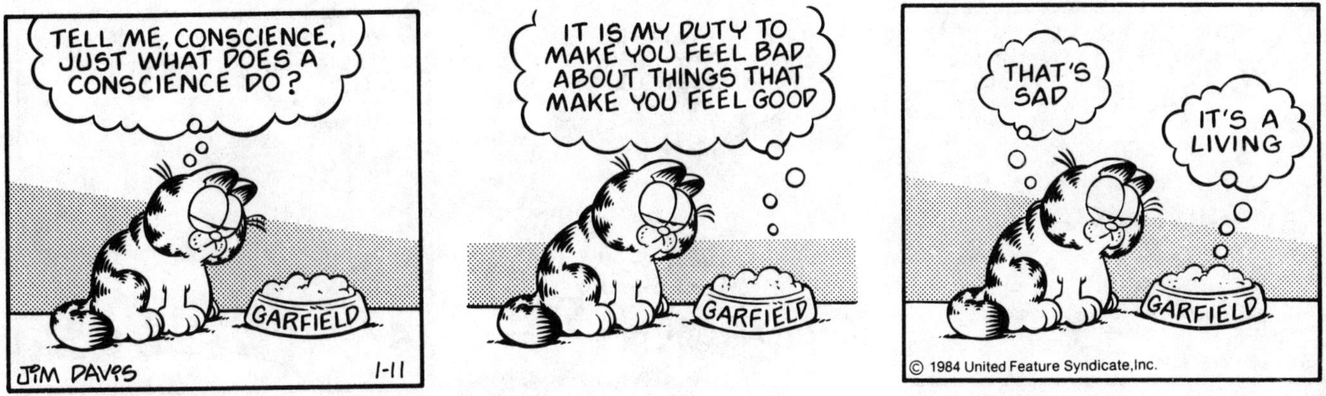
TELL ME, CONSCIENCE, JUST WHAT DOES A CONSCIENCE DO?
JIM DAVIS
1-11
IT IS MY DUTY TO MAKE YOU FEEL BAD ABOUT THINGS THAT MAKE YOU FEEL GOOD
GARFIELD
THAT'S SAD
IT'S A LIVING
© 1984 United Feature Syndicate, Inc.

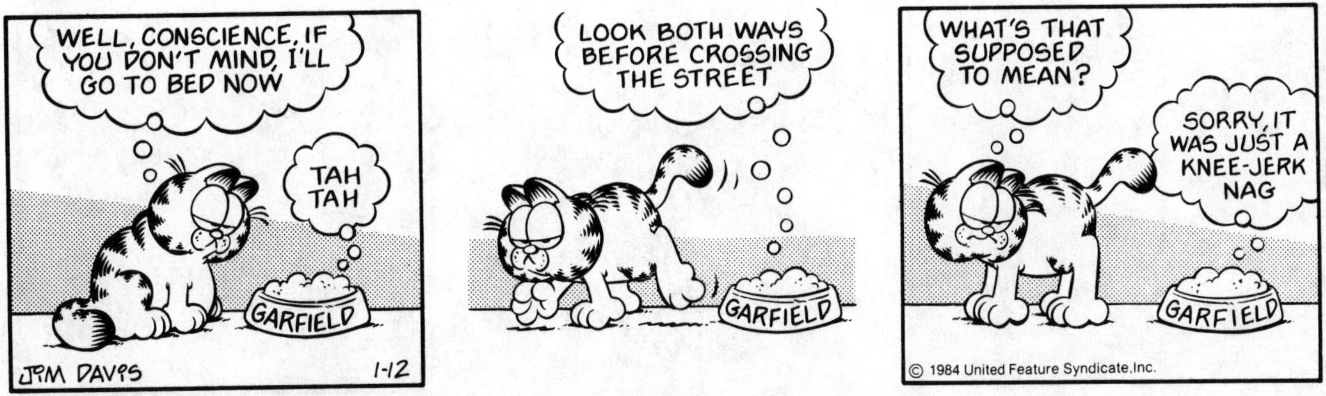
WELL, CONSCIENCE, IF YOU DON'T MIND, I'LL GO TO BED NOW
TAH TAH
JIM DAVIS
1-12
LOOK BOTH WAYS BEFORE CROSSING THE STREET
GARFIELD
WHAT'S THAT SUPPOSED TO MEAN?
SORRY, IT WAS JUST A KNEE-JERK NAG
© 1984 United Feature Syndicate, Inc.

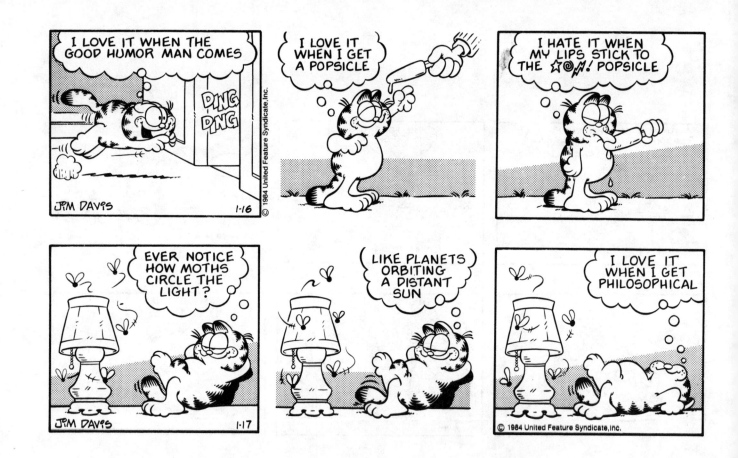

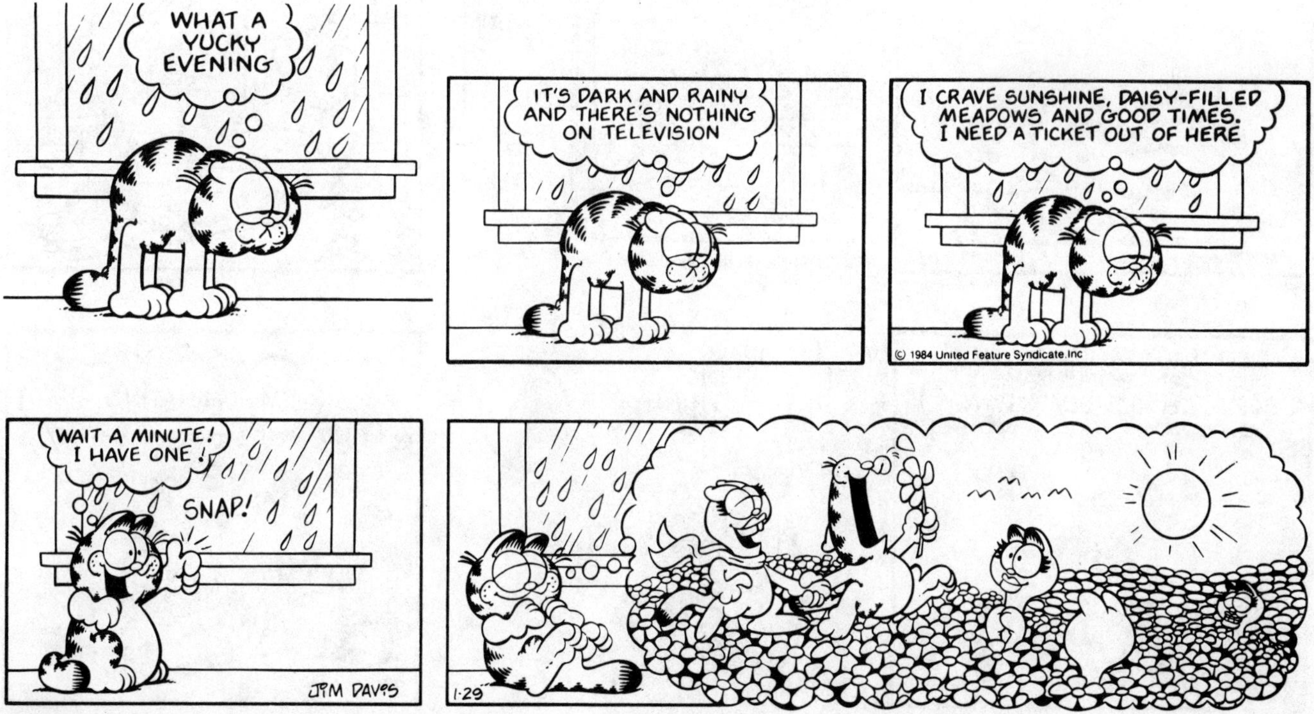
WHAT A YUCKY EVENING
IT'S DARK AND RAINY AND THERE'S NOTHING ON TELEVISION
I CRAVE SUNSHINE, DAISY-FILLED MEADOWS AND GOOD TIMES. I NEED A TICKET OUT OF HERE
© 1984 United Feature Syndicate, Inc
WAIT A MINUTE! I HAVE ONE!
SNAP!
JIM DAVIS
1-29

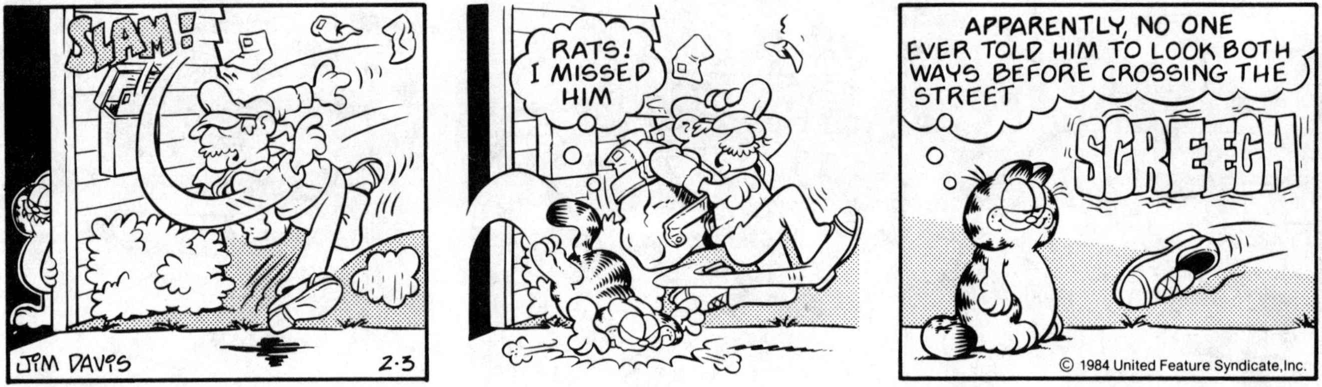
SLAM!
JIM DAVIS
2-3
RATS! I MISSED HIM
APPARENTLY, NO ONE EVER TOLD HIM TO LOOK BOTH WAYS BEFORE CROSSING THE STREET
SCREECH
© 1984 United Feature Syndicate, Inc.

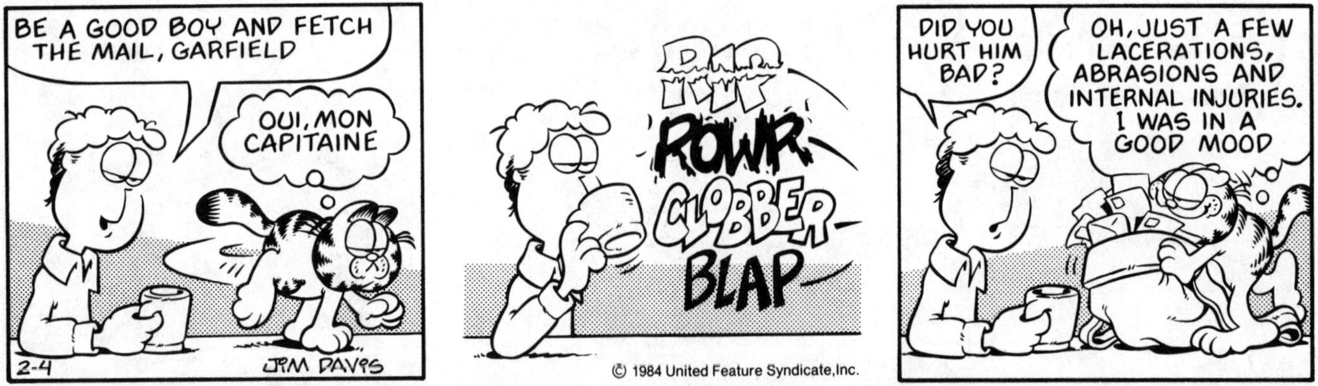
BE A GOOD BOY AND FETCH THE MAIL, GARFIELD
OUI, MON CAPITAINE
2-4
JIM DAVIS
ROWR
CLOBBER
BLAP
© 1984 United Feature Syndicate, Inc.
DID YOU HURT HIM BAD?
OH, JUST A FEW LACERATIONS, ABRASIONS AND INTERNAL INJURIES. I WAS IN A GOOD MOOD

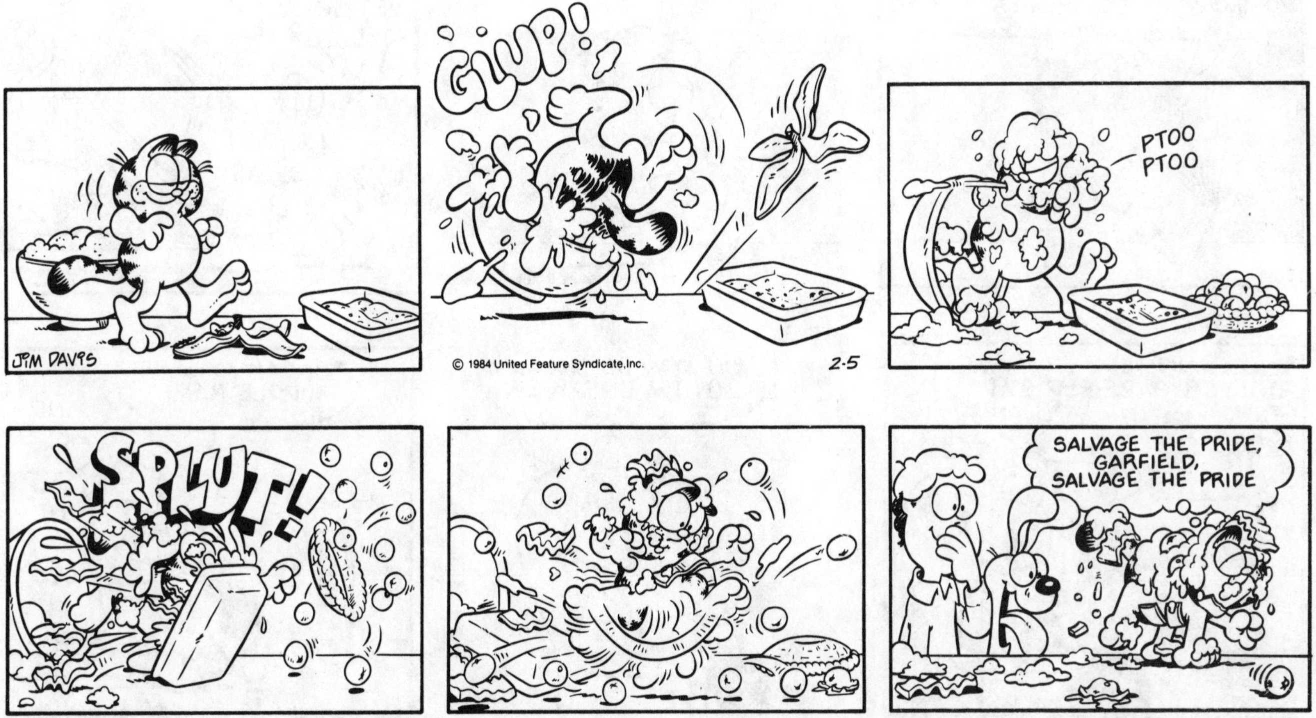
JIM DAVIS
GLUP!
© 1984 United Feature Syndicate, Inc.
2-5
PTOO PTOO
SPLUT!
SALVAGE THE PRIDE, GARFIELD, SALVAGE THE PRIDE

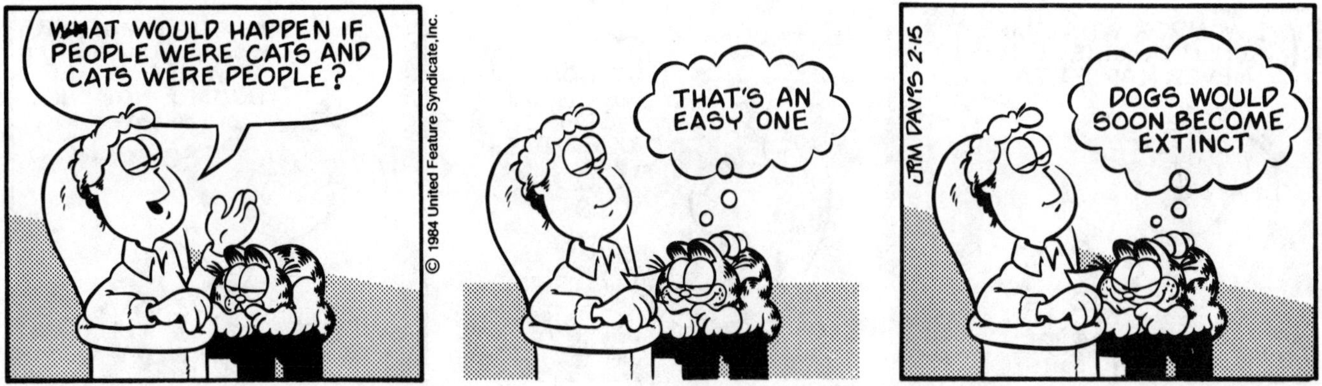
WHAT WOULD HAPPEN IF PEOPLE WERE CATS AND CATS WERE PEOPLE?
© 1984 United Feature Syndicate,Inc.
THAT'S AN EASY ONE
JPM DAVPS 2-15
DOGS WOULD SOON BECOME EXTINCT

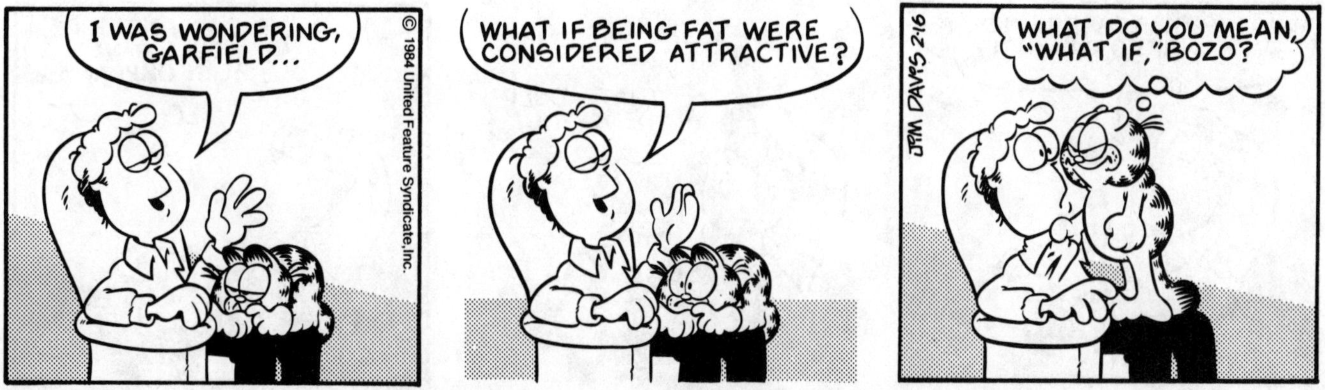
I WAS WONDERING, GARFIELD...
© 1984 United Feature Syndicate,Inc.
WHAT IF BEING FAT WERE CONSIDERED ATTRACTIVE?
JPM DAVPS 2-16
WHAT DO YOU MEAN, "WHAT IF," BOZO?

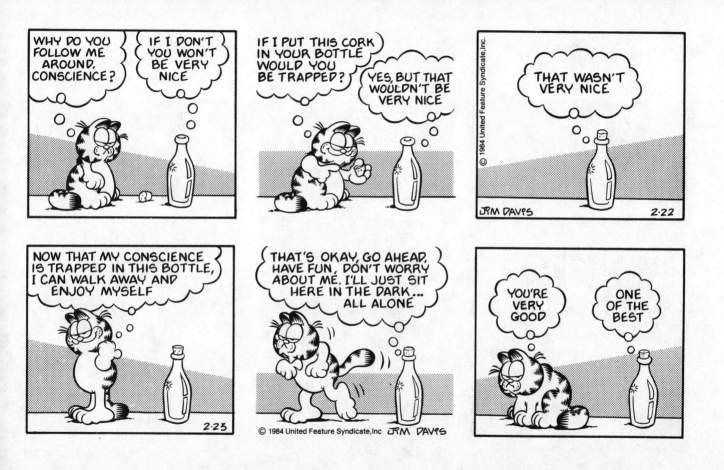

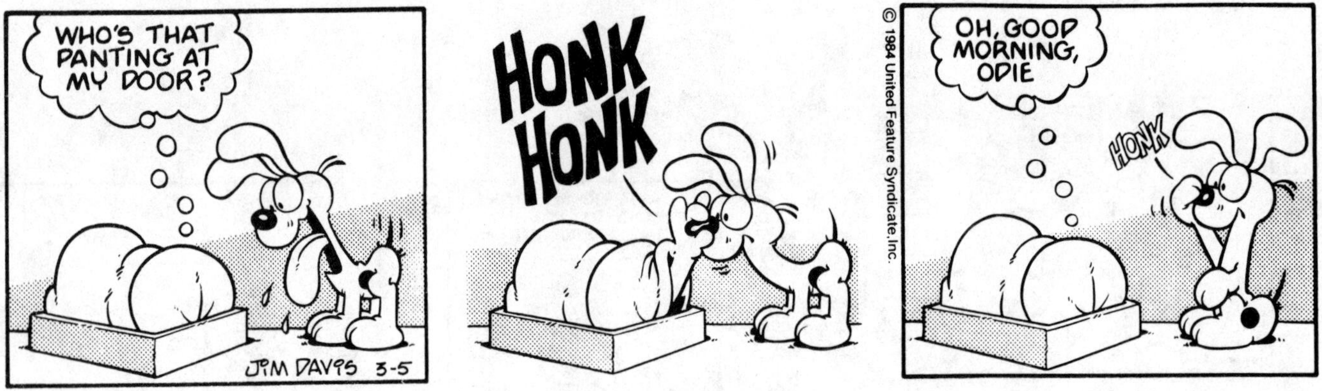
WHO'S THAT PANTING AT MY DOOR?
JIM DAVIS 3-5
HONK HONK
© 1984 United Feature Syndicate, Inc.
OH, GOOD MORNING, ODIE
HONK

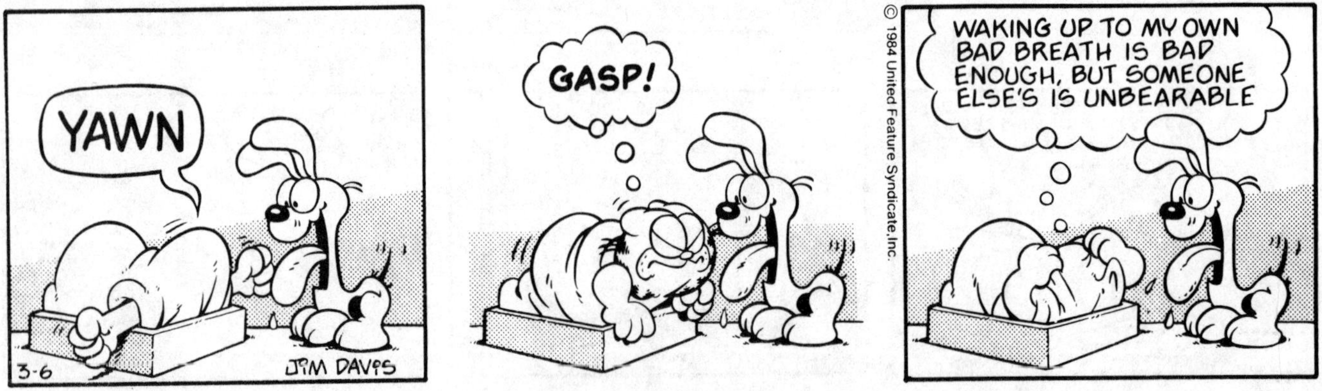
YAWN
3-6
JIM DAVIS
GASP!
© 1984 United Feature Syndicate, Inc.
WAKING UP TO MY OWN BAD BREATH IS BAD ENOUGH, BUT SOMEONE ELSE'S IS UNBEARABLE

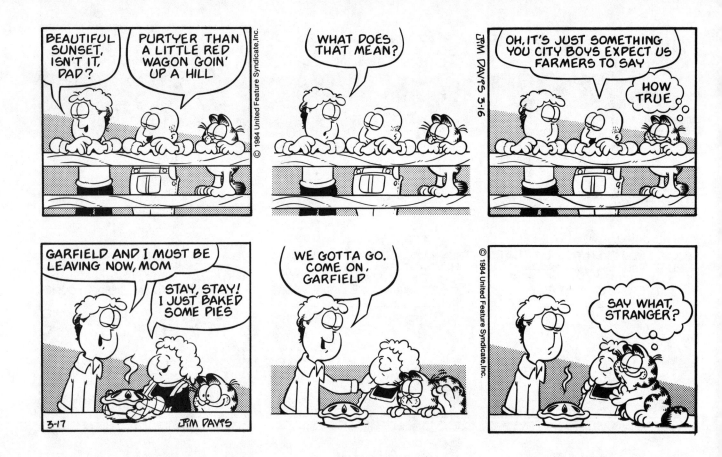

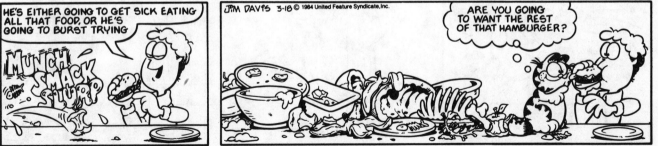

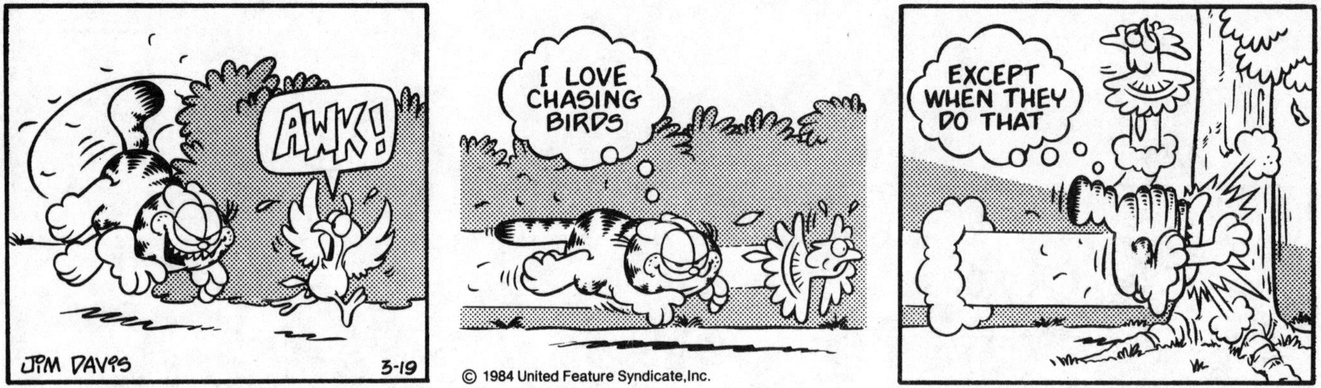
AWK!
JIM DAVIS
3-19
I LOVE CHASING BIRDS
EXCEPT WHEN THEY DO THAT

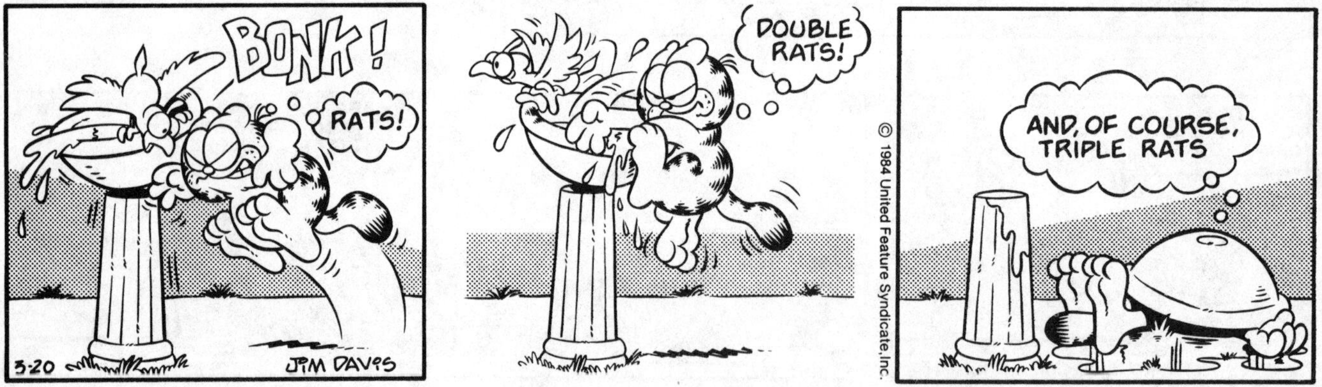
BONK!
RATS!
3-20
JIM DAVIS
DOUBLE RATS!
AND, OF COURSE, TRIPLE RATS

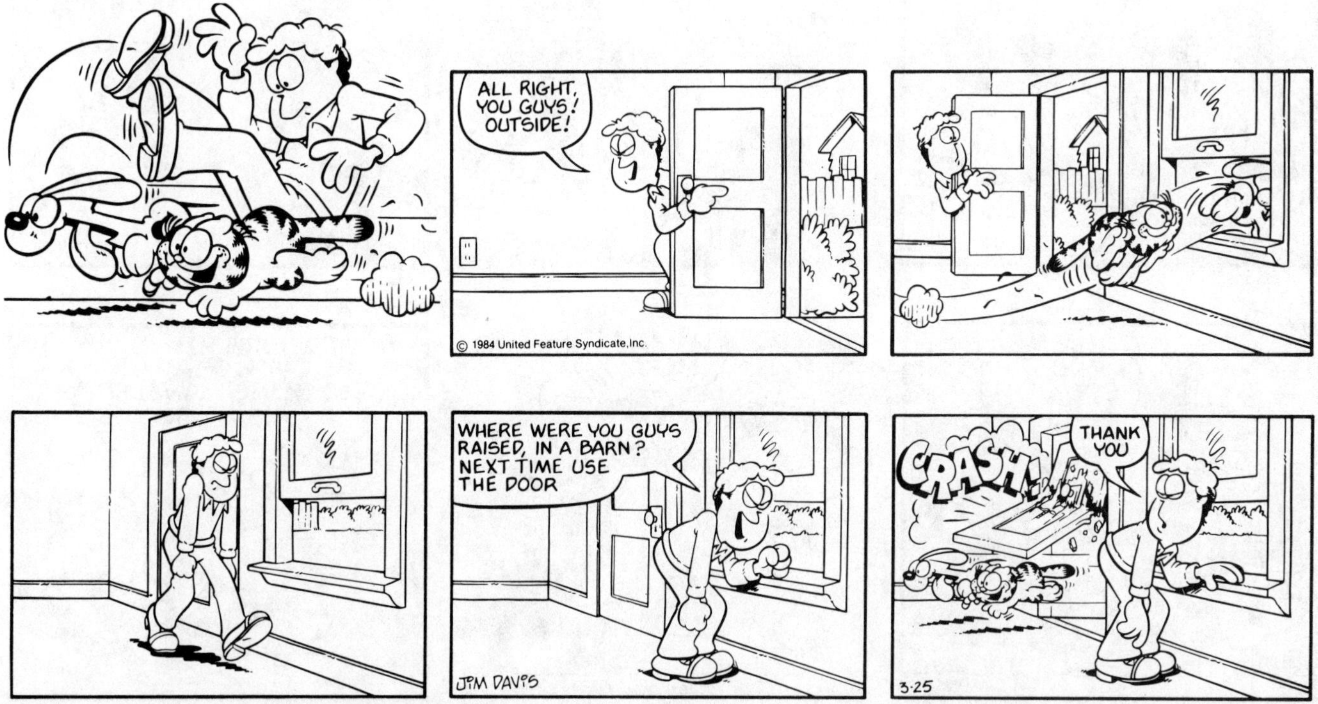

ALL RIGHT, YOU GUYS! OUTSIDE!
© 1984 United Feature Syndicate, Inc.
WHERE WERE YOU GUYS RAISED, IN A BARN? NEXT TIME USE THE DOOR
JIM DAVIS
CRASH!
THANK YOU
3-25

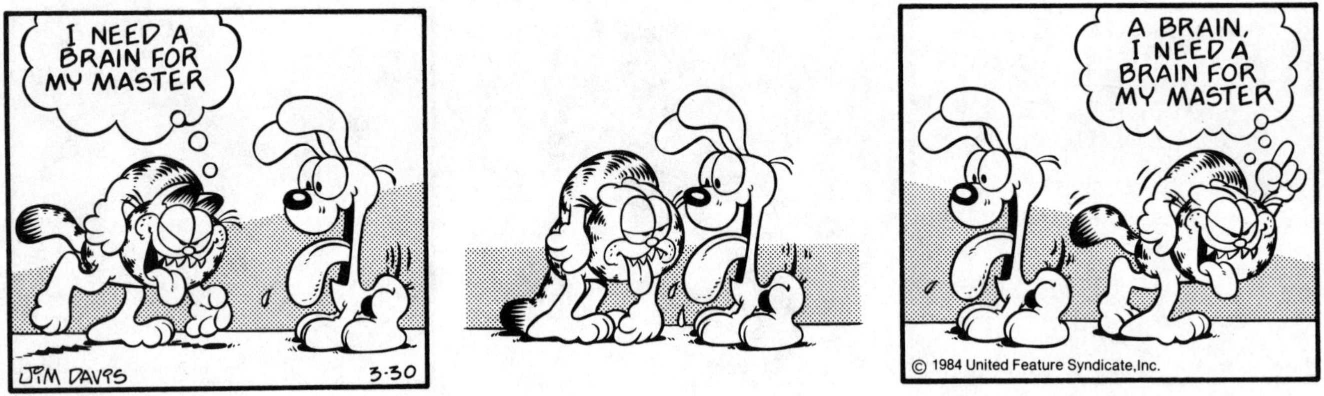
I NEED A BRAIN FOR MY MASTER
JIM DAVIS
3-30
A BRAIN, I NEED A BRAIN FOR MY MASTER
© 1984 United Feature Syndicate,Inc.

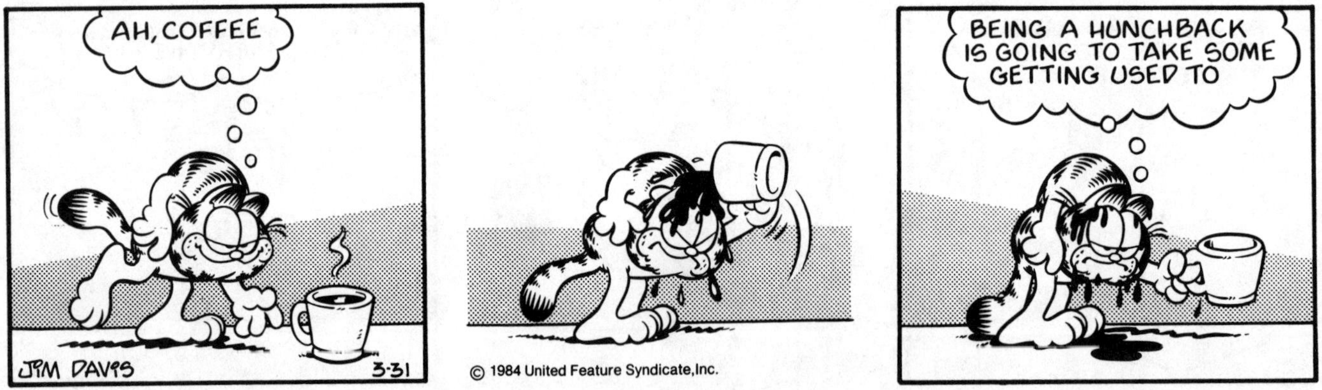
AH, COFFEE
JIM DAVIS
3-31
© 1984 United Feature Syndicate,Inc.
BEING A HUNCHBACK IS GOING TO TAKE SOME GETTING USED TO

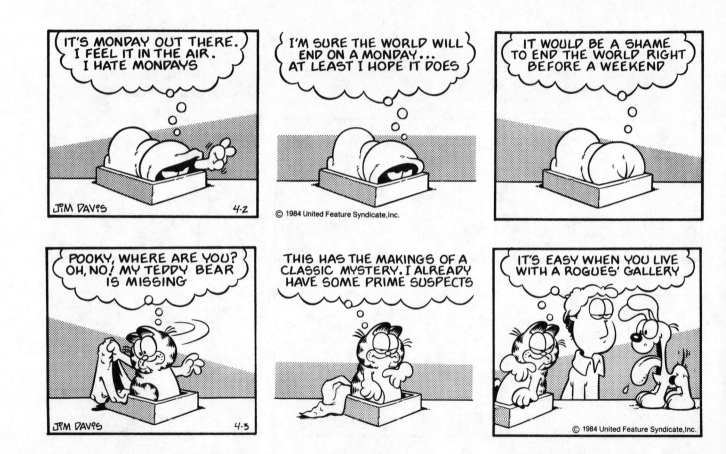

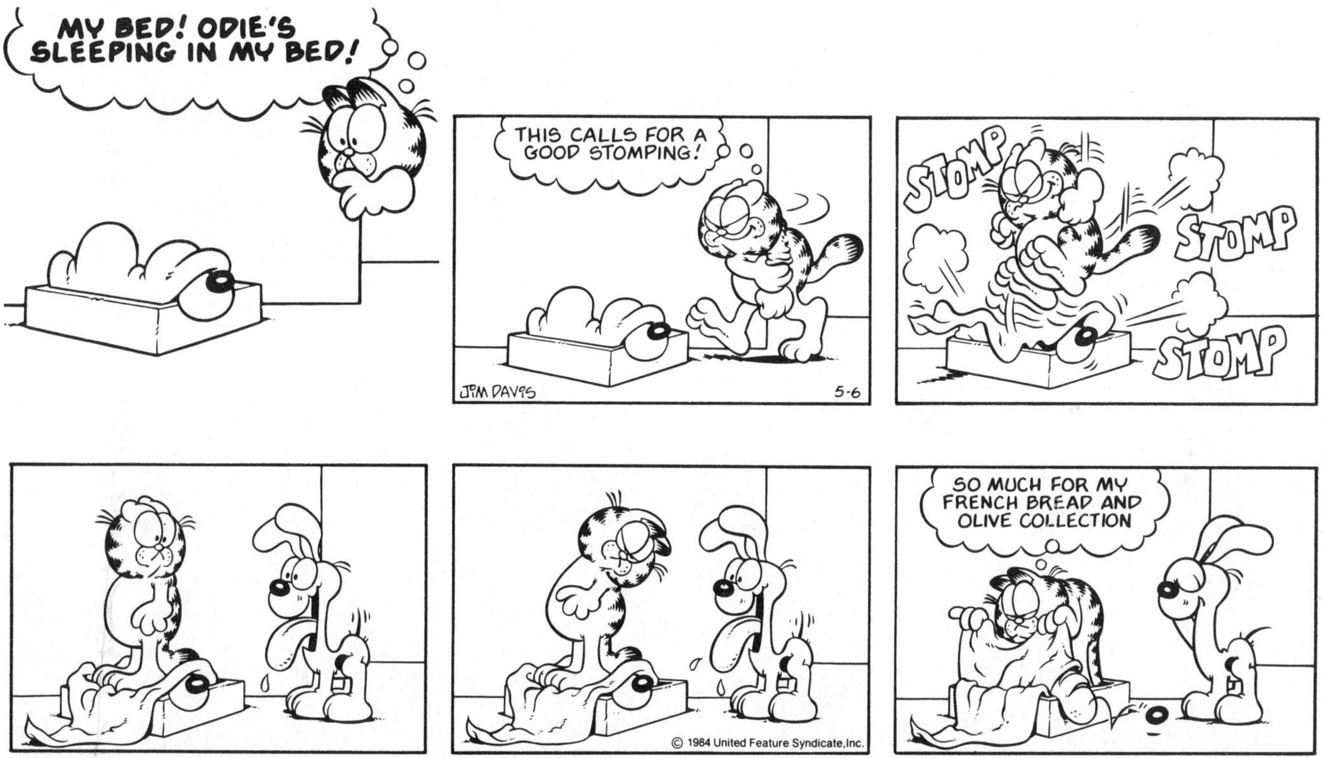
MY BED! ODIE'S SLEEPING IN MY BED!
THIS CALLS FOR A GOOD STOMPING!
JIM DAVIS
5-6
STOMP
STOMP
STOMP
© 1984 United Feature Syndicate, Inc.
SO MUCH FOR MY FRENCH BREAD AND OLIVE COLLECTION

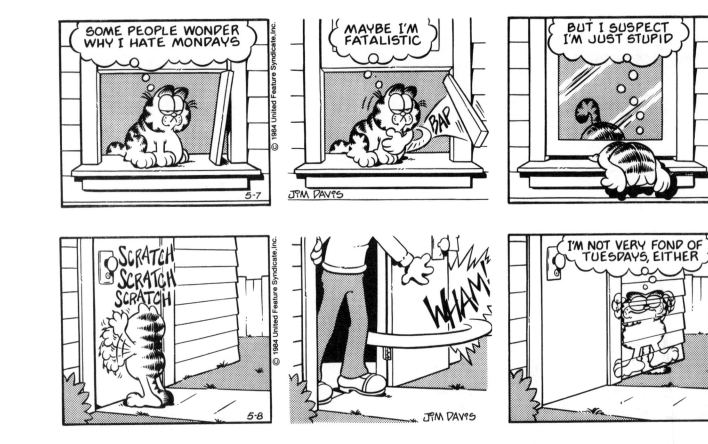

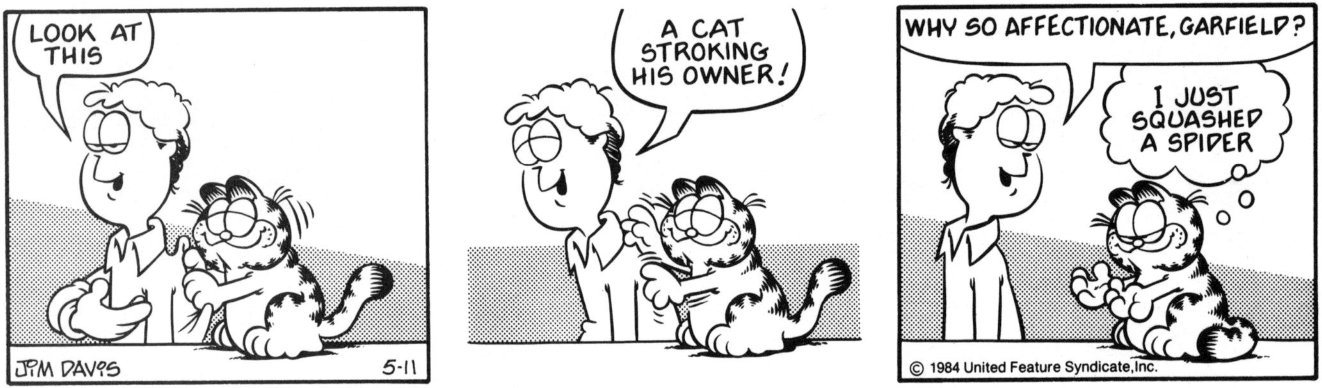
LOOK AT THIS
A CAT STROKING HIS OWNER!
WHY SO AFFECTIONATE, GARFIELD?
I JUST SQUASHED A SPIDER
JIM DAVIS
5-11
© 1984 United Feature Syndicate, Inc.

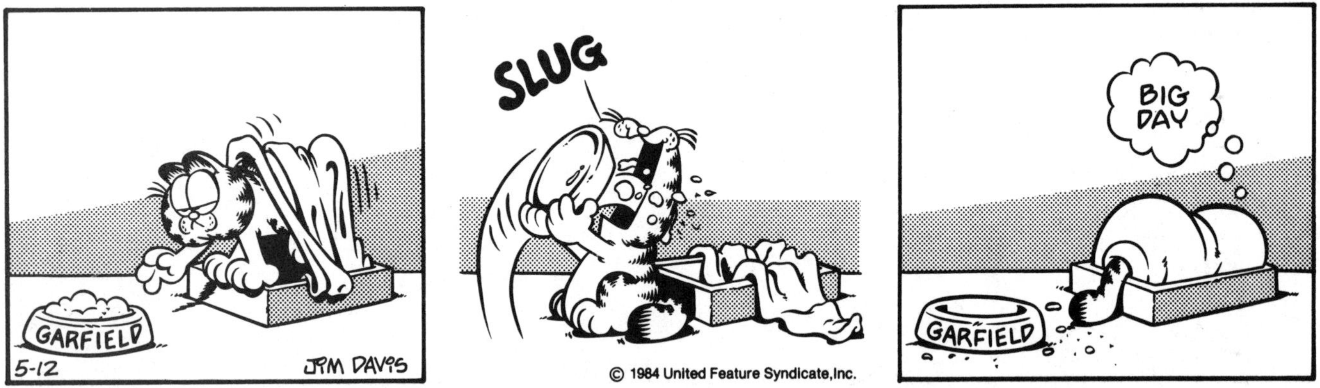
GARFIELD
5-12
JIM DAVIS
SLUG
© 1984 United Feature Syndicate, Inc.
BIG DAY
GARFIELD

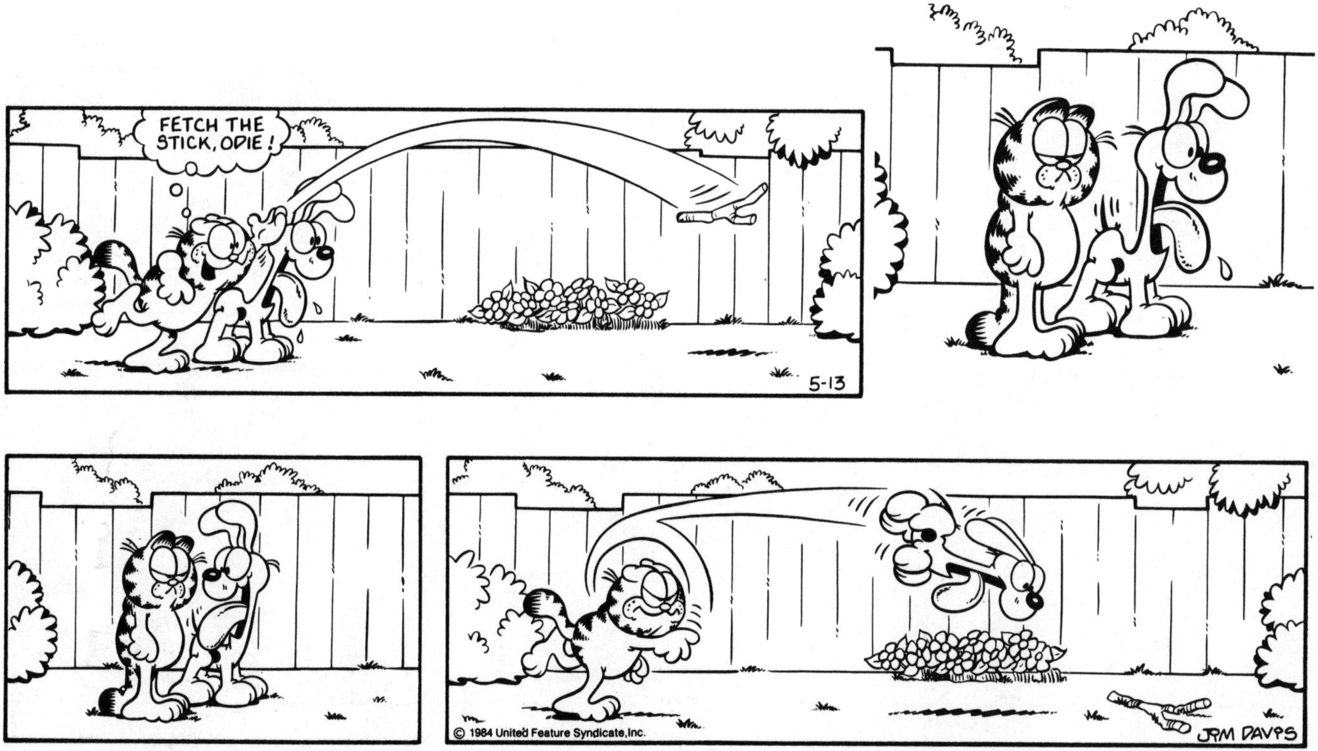
FETCH THE STICK, ODIE!
5-13
© 1984 United Feature Syndicate, Inc.
JIM DAVIS

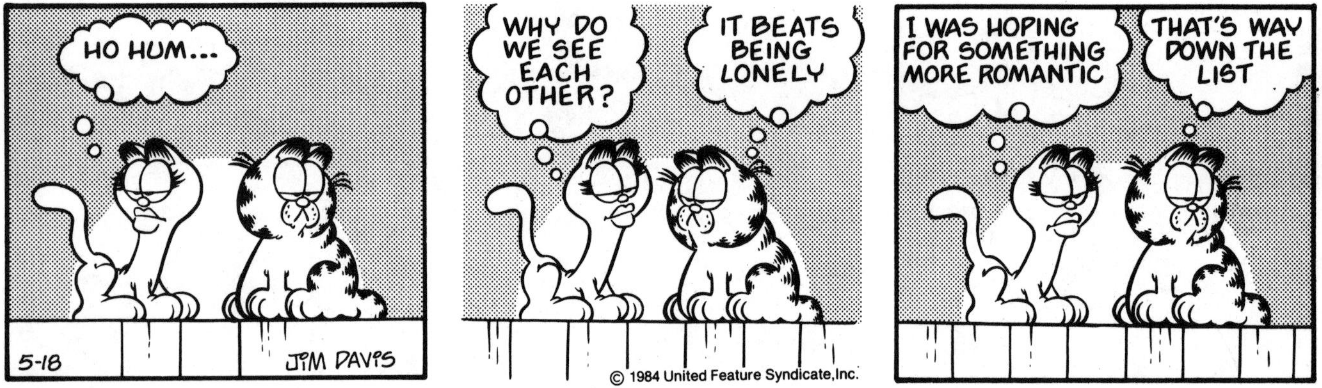
HO HUM...
5-18
JIM DAVIS
WHY DO WE SEE EACH OTHER?
IT BEATS BEING LONELY
© 1984 United Feature Syndicate, Inc.
I WAS HOPING FOR SOMETHING MORE ROMANTIC
THAT'S WAY DOWN THE LIST

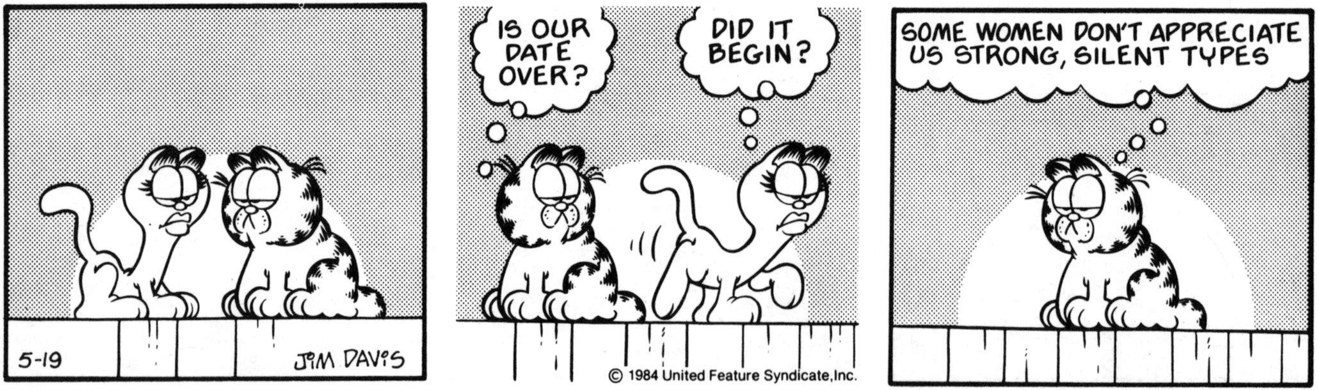
5-19
JIM DAVIS
IS OUR DATE OVER?
DID IT BEGIN?
© 1984 United Feature Syndicate, Inc.
SOME WOMEN DON'T APPRECIATE US STRONG, SILENT TYPES

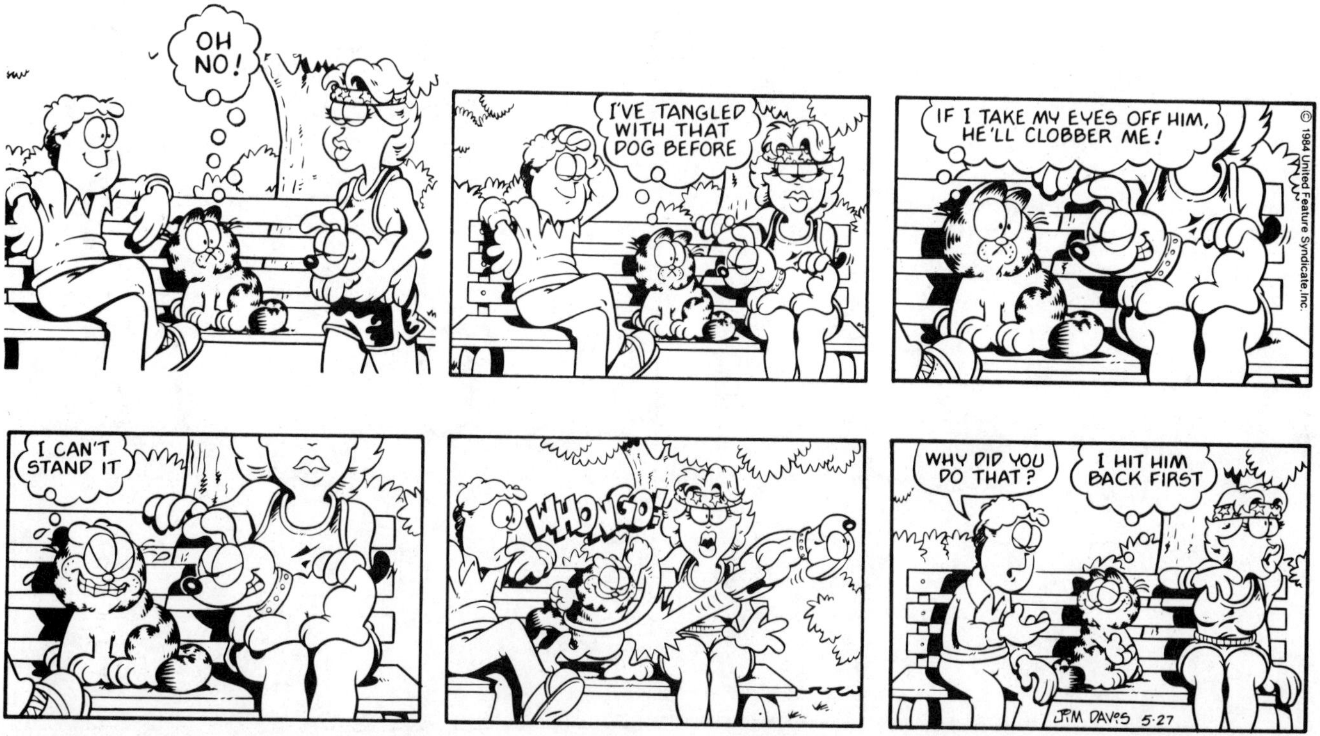

OH NO!
I'VE TANGLED WITH THAT DOG BEFORE
IF I TAKE MY EYES OFF HIM, HE'LL CLOBBER ME!
© 1984 United Feature Syndicate, Inc.
I CAN'T STAND IT
WHONGO!
WHY DID YOU DO THAT?
I HIT HIM BACK FIRST
JIM DAVIS 5-27

Garfield's Loves & Hates

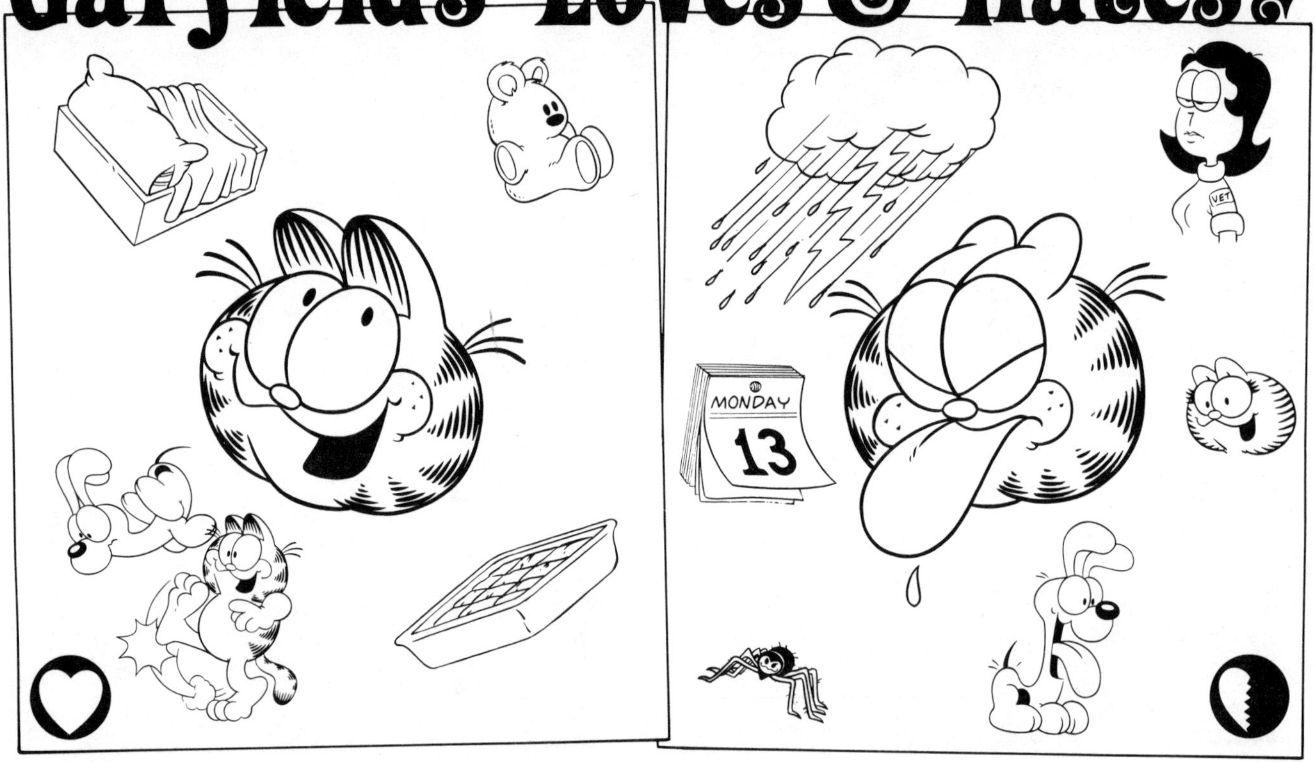

VET
MONDAY
13